LOOKING AT
SPACE

Written by **Ian Graham**

TWO-CAN

First published in Great Britain in 1991 by
Two-Can Publishing Ltd
27 Cowper Street
London EC2A 4AP

Copyright © Two-Can Publishing Ltd, 1991

Text copyright © Ian Graham, 1991
Editorial and Design by Lionheart Books, London
Editor: Denny Robson Picture Research: Jennie Karrach
Media conversion: Peter MacDonald, Una Macnamara and Vanessa Hersey
Studio Artwork: Radius

Printed and bound in Hong Kong

This impression published 1991 in association with Scholastic Publications Ltd.

2 4 6 8 10 9 7 5 3

All rights reserved. No part of this publication may be reproduced,
stored in a retrieval system, or transmitted in any form or by any
means, electronic, mechanical, photocopying, recording or otherwise,
without prior written permission of the copyright owner.

The JUMP! logo and the word JUMP! are registered trade marks.

British Library Cataloguing in Publication Data
Graham, Ian
    Looking at Space
    1. Outer space
    1. Title
    523

ISBN 1-85434-083-2

Photographic Credits:
p.4 Ann Ronan Picture Library. p.5 Royal Observatory, Edinburgh. p.9 Michael Holford Picture Library. p.10, 11-12 Robin Scagell. p.13 NASA/Standard Picture Library.
p.14, 15 Royal Observatory, Edinburgh. p.16 NAT Radio Astronomical Observatory/Astronomical Society of the Pacific. p.16-17 ZEFA Photo Library. p.18 NASA.
p.19 NASA. p.20 Martin Marietta/Ian Graham. p.21 Julian Baum. p.22 NASA/Spacecharts. p.30 Royal Greenwich Observatory. p.31 US Naval Observatory.
Cover photo NASA.

Illustration Credits:
All illustrations by Chris Forsey and Peter Bull except those on pages 24-28, which are by Graham Humphreys of Virgil Pomfret Artists.

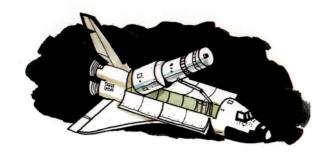

CONTENTS

Ancient thoughts	4
Constellations	6
Famous astronomers	8
Telescopes	10
What you might see	12
Observatories	14
Looking further	16
Telescopes in space	18
Space probes	20
Moon mobile	22
A trip to the observatory	24
True or false?	29
Glossary	30
Index	32

All words marked in **bold** can be found in the glossary

ANCIENT THOUGHTS

For thousands of years people have wondered what the stars are and how they move. Some people, especially leaders of early religions, studied the stars carefully and became expert in predicting their movements. Many believed that if seasons could be predicted by studying the sky, then perhaps everyday events could be predicted too. This is called astrology.

The scientific study of the stars and planets is called astronomy. The greatest of the early astronomers were the Greeks. They believed that the stars and the planets revolved around the Earth because they were fixed to crystal spheres that were driven by machines. These incorrect ideas lasted for over 1,000 years.

DID YOU KNOW?

Claudius Ptolemaeus was a famous Greek astronomer who lived in the second century. Like many people at that time, he believed (wrongly) that the Earth was at the centre of the Universe, with the Sun, the Moon, the planets and the stars all revolving around it. This is called the Ptolemaic System.

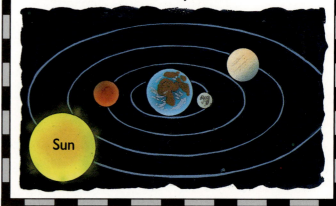

◀ Early astronomers believed that if they could break through the crystal sphere of the sky, they would be able to see the machines behind it that make the Universe work.

▶ The sheer numbers of stars in the sky has always amazed people. New stars are forming all the time. This picture shows the Trifid **Nebula**, also called **M20**. Stars are forming in its bright middle region.

CONSTELLATIONS

Ancient astronomers divided the sky into groups of stars called constellations. They claimed to be able to see the shapes of people and animals in the patterns of the stars, and so they named the constellations after the heroes and animals in their myths and legends. As the Earth revolves around the Sun, the constellations move across the sky.

Different constellations appear in the sky at different times of the year, but each constellation reappears in the east at the same time in the following year.

The stars in a constellation are not actually close together. They just appear to be close together when viewed from Earth. Some are much closer to the Earth than others.

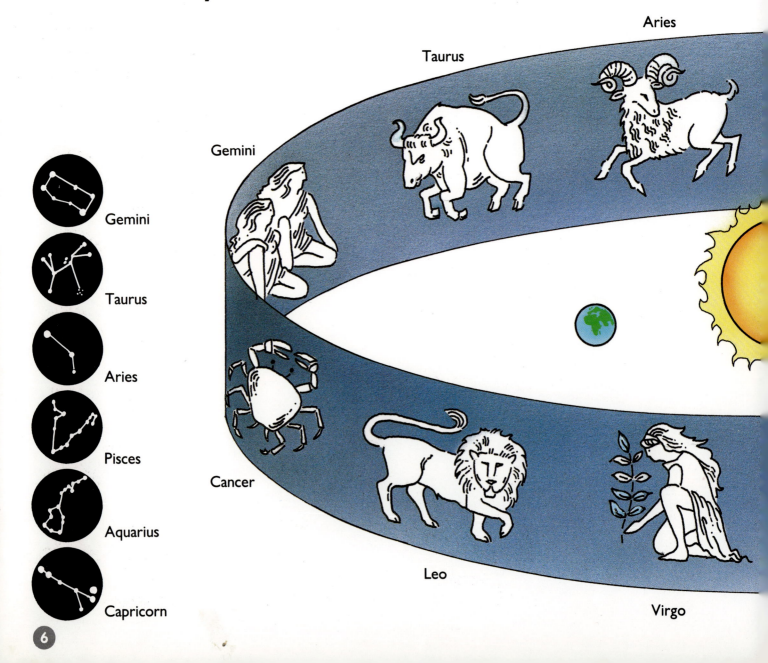

DID YOU KNOW?

The ancient Egyptians worshipped the Sun as a god called Ra, who is drawn as a hawk, or a man with a hawk's head.

Modern astronomers still use the ancient constellation names because they are useful as signposts in the sky for describing where a star or a planet can be found.

The paths of the Sun, the Moon and the planets form a wide band across the sky that passes through 12 constellations called the zodiac. These are known not only by their names but also by special signs given to them by astrologers. They are called the signs of the zodiac.

◀ The 12 constellations of the zodiac lie in a band around the sky. Astrologers use them to produce plans of future events, called horoscopes.

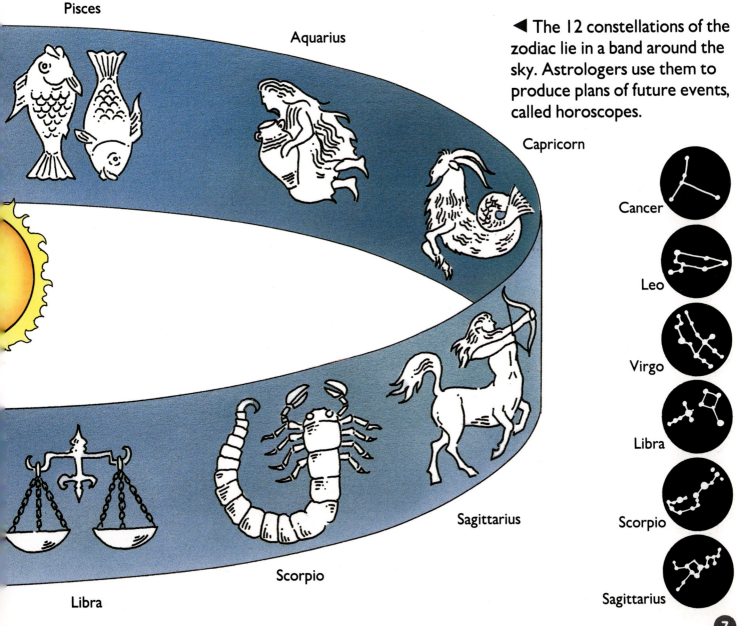

FAMOUS ASTRONOMERS

Our understanding of the Universe has advanced slowly over many centuries. Each new generation of astronomers studies the work done by all the astronomers of the past and builds upon it to make new discoveries and develop new theories to explain what they observe. A few astronomers made important discoveries that changed the course of astronomy.

The idea that Earth was the centre of the Universe was challenged by people such as Copernicus and Galileo in the 16th and 17th centuries. Galileo also made some of the earliest telescopes, providing astronomers with a new view of the heavens. A man called Kepler developed laws of motion to describe how the planets move. Sir Isaac Newton, the greatest scientist of his time, developed a theory to explain the force of gravity between the Sun and the planets.

▲ Newton showed a new type of telescope called a reflector to the Royal Society in London in 1671. It magnified images using a curved metal mirror only 2.5cm (1 inch) across.

◄ Herschel's giant telescope, built in 1789, was used until 1816. The telescope tube was tilted up and down by pulling on ropes, and it was rotated by pushing its wooden base round.

DID YOU KNOW?

● When Copernicus and later Galileo suggested that the Sun was at the centre of our planetary system and not the Earth, they faced great opposition from the Church and from other scientists.

Copernicus 1473-1543   Galileo 1564-1642

● Johannes Kepler was the first person to realise that the planets travelled in paths that are not circular, but are flattened circles called ellipses.

Kepler 1571-1630

● Many mathematical problems in astronomy were solved by Sir Isaac Newton and published in his book known as the *Principia* in 1687.

● Sir William Herschel discovered Uranus in 1781 and measured the length of a day on Mars to within a few seconds.

Newton 1642-1727   Herschel 1738-1822

TELESCOPES

Telescopes enable astronomers to see objects in the sky that are too small or faint to see with the eyes alone. Thousands of people all over the world use telescopes at home to make astronomical observations as a hobby. Professional astronomers usually work with bigger telescopes housed inside specially designed buildings called observatories. The largest telescopes can see the most distant objects.

▶ Astronomy is one of the few areas of scientific observation that ordinary people can still contribute to at home.

OBSERVING HINT

It is not essential to have a telescope to make astronomical observations. A pair of binoculars can be used. Binoculars are marked according to how powerful they are. A 7×50 pair magnifies seven times and the lenses at the opposite end from the eyepieces are 50 mm (2 inches) across. These binoculars are powerful enough to be used for astronomy.

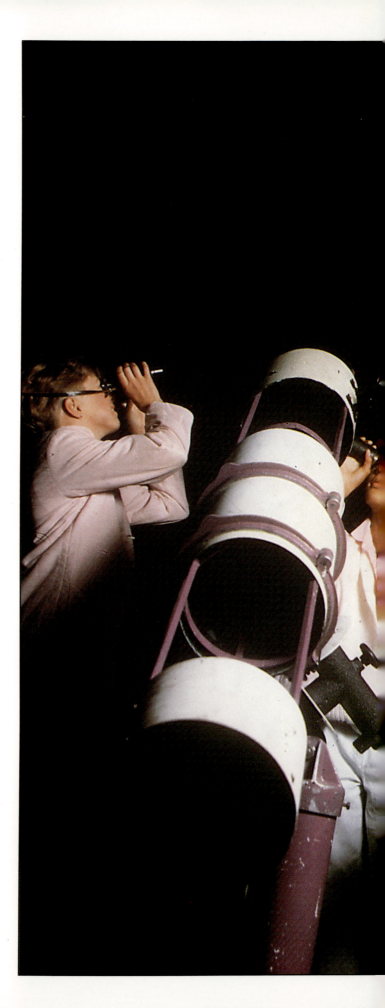

Telescopes must be able to move so that they can be pointed at different parts of the sky. To take a photograph of the image in the telescope, as they often do in observatories, it may be necessary to keep the telescope pointed at the same star for several minutes or hours. A star appears to move as the Earth spins and this would blur a photograph. To keep the star in view and ensure that the photograph is sharply focused, the telescope has to move or 'track' the star. This is usually done with electric motors.

◄ Amateur astronomers – children study the night sky from a garden using a telescope and binoculars.

TELESCOPES

There are two types of telescope, refractors and reflectors. A refractor uses lenses to collect light and magnify the image. In a reflector, a curved mirror is used instead of a lens to collect light from the image and magnify it.

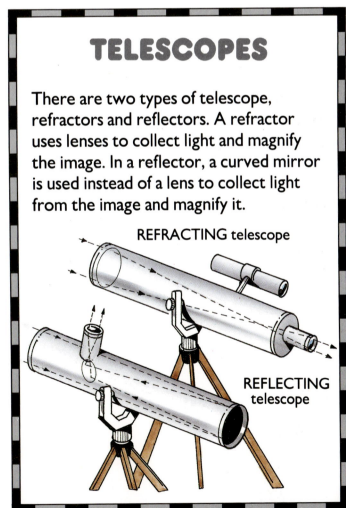

REFRACTING telescope

REFLECTING telescope

WHAT YOU MIGHT SEE

NEVER look at the Sun or point a telescope or binoculars at the Sun. It is so bright that it can damage your eyes permanently. Stars other than the Sun are so far away that they are never bigger than points of light and they are safe to look at.

The biggest object in the night sky is the Moon. It is actually a fraction of the size of a planet or a star, but it is so much closer to the Earth that it looks bigger than everything else in the sky. Binoculars or a telescope show **craters** on the Moon's surface very clearly. Some of the planets can also be seen, especially Jupiter and Saturn. Saturn's rings may be visible if they are tilted towards the Earth.

DID YOU KNOW?

● Sometimes streaks of light appear in the night sky for a moment. These are shooting stars or meteors. They are grains of dust from space burning up as they speed into the **atmosphere**.

● Stars twinkle because light from them is twisted this way and that as it passes through the Earth's atmosphere.

● At first glance the stars seem to be white points, but many are blue or red. Blue stars are hot and young. White or yellow stars, like our Sun, are in the middle of their lifespan and red stars are near the end of their lives.

● Some objects in the sky are not stars at all but **galaxies** containing hundreds of millions of stars. Through a powerful telescope, they appear as swirling spirals of light.

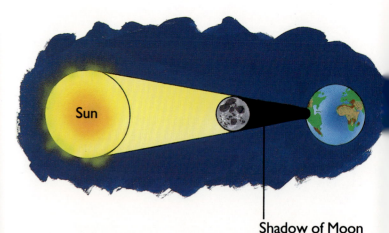

Shadow of Moon

▲ If the Moon comes between the Sun and the Earth, casting a shadow on the Earth, this is a solar **eclipse**. The Moon may cover the whole Sun, or a ring of sunlight may shine around the Moon, as in the photo. In a partial eclipse only part of the Sun is covered.

MOON FACTS

● The Moon spins round once in the same time that it takes it to revolve around the Earth. This is why the Moon always shows the same side to Earth, as above.

● We see the Moon because it reflects sunlight to Earth. Its shape appears to change as the Sun, Earth and Moon move and different parts of the Moon are lit up.

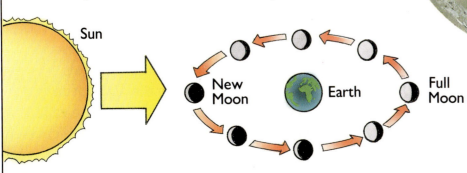

1 The Sea of Moisture
2 The Sea of Clouds
3 The Ocean of Storms
4 Copernicus Crater
5 The Sea of Rains
6 The Sea of Cold
7 The Sea of Serenity
8 The Sea of Vapours
9 The Sea of Tranquility
10 The Sea of Crises
11 The Sea of Fertility
12 The Sea of Nectar

OBSERVATORIES

Observatories are buildings specially designed to house telescopes. Until the twentieth century, observatories were built within easy reach of the astronomers who used them – near a university, for example. Cities are now so bright at night that their light is reflected by the dust in the air into the telescopes. This makes it difficult to see faint objects in the night sky. Observatories are now built high up on mountain tops where they are above most of the pollution, dust and water vapour in the atmosphere.

DID YOU KNOW?

● The Royal Observatory of 1675 in Greenwich, London, the starting point for world time-charts, had to be moved because of the bright lighting and air pollution in Greenwich. It is now on top of a mountain in the Canary Islands.

● Some telescopes are now controlled by computers down a telephone line. Astronomers can control a telescope from computers in other countries.

◀ The UK 1.2 m across (4 foot) Schmidt telescope can be seen through the open doors of its observatory. Telescopes normally have a very narrow angle of view. The Schmidt telescope invented by Bernhardt Schmidt in the 1930s is designed to produce images of large areas of the sky.

▶ The 3.9 m across (13 foot) Anglo-Australian telescope. This telescope swivels between the arms of an enormous horseshoe called the South Bearing, which itself swivels. The huge mirror is at the bottom of the framework.

LOOKING FURTHER

Of all the energy streaming towards the Earth from space, only the narrow band of visible light and a narrow band of radio waves reach the Earth's surface. The rest is blocked by the atmosphere. Optical telescopes are used to study visible light from space.

▼ This is an image received by a radio telescope. The different strengths of radio signals are shown in different colours.

Radio telescopes are used to study radio signals from space. Most radio telescopes are metal dishes designed to collect as much energy as possible and reflect it up to a radio receiver suspended above the dish. Radio telescopes have discovered some of the most distant objects in the Universe, the immensely bright yet very small objects called **quasars**.

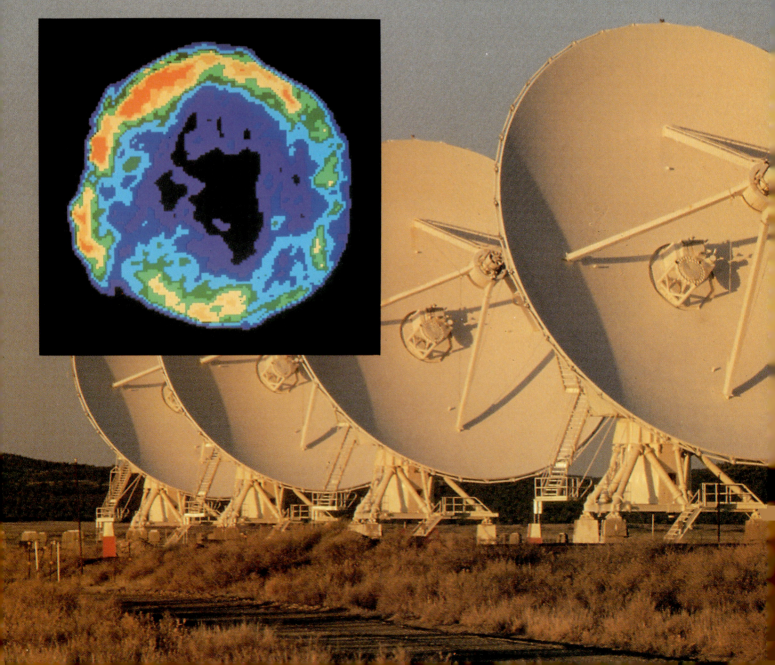

▼ Several small radio telescopes can produce the same results as a single large one. As the Earth rotates, the dishes are carried round with it in a circle. A computer combines the signals from all the dishes and produces a picture.

TELESCOPES IN SPACE

The Earth's atmosphere distorts the images of distant stars and galaxies that we receive through telescopes on the surface of the Earth. Telescopes placed above the atmosphere can receive much sharper images. Astronomy from space began with the Orbiting Solar Observatory OSO-1.

The OSO-1 was launched in 1962 by the United States to study the Sun. A telescope carried by the US Skylab also studied the Sun in the 1970s. Orbiting observatories can receive infra-red, ultra-violet and X-ray energy that cannot be received on Earth because of the atmosphere.

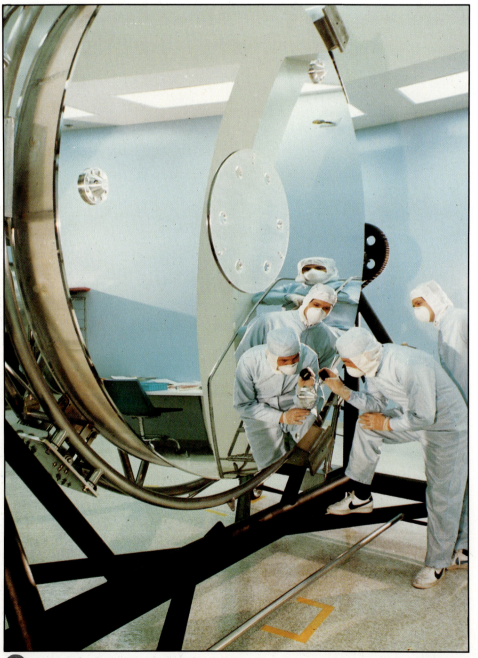

◀ Scientists examine the main mirror of the Hubble Space Telescope. In April 1990, the US Space Shuttle *Discovery* was launched with the telescope on board. On the second day of the mission the telescope was eased out of the Shuttle's cargo bay and into space. There, the space telescope will allow astronomers to study details seven times smaller than the smallest ones currently visible from Earth.

▶ In this artist's impression of the Space Telescope, the solar panels that produce the telescope's electrical power are clearly visible on each side of the telescope tube. The door that protects the telescope's mirror has been swung open.

SHUTTLE LAUNCH

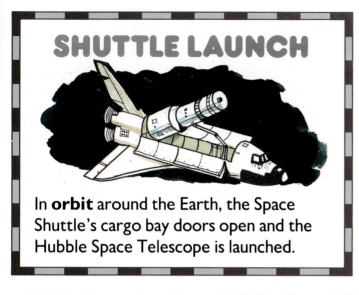

In **orbit** around the Earth, the Space Shuttle's cargo bay doors open and the Hubble Space Telescope is launched.

The Hubble Space Telescope, named after the US astronomer Edwin Hubble, is the biggest space observatory ever built. It weighs 11 tonnes and is 13.1 m (43 feet) long and 4.3 m (14 feet) across. Its 2.4 m (8 foot) wide mirror is the smoothest ever made. It is expected to be able to see objects 14 billion light-years away that are 50 times fainter than can be seen by telescopes on the ground.

SPACE PROBES

Since 1961 unmanned space probes have flown past or landed on every planet in the **Solar System** except Pluto. They have provided valuable information about the Sun and planets that could not have been learned using ground-based instruments. Further missions to Mars, Venus, Jupiter and Saturn are planned for the 1990s.

▶ An impression of the Voyager 2 space probe minutes from its closest approach to Uranus in 1986. The Magellan space probe (inset) ready for its journey to Venus in May 1989.

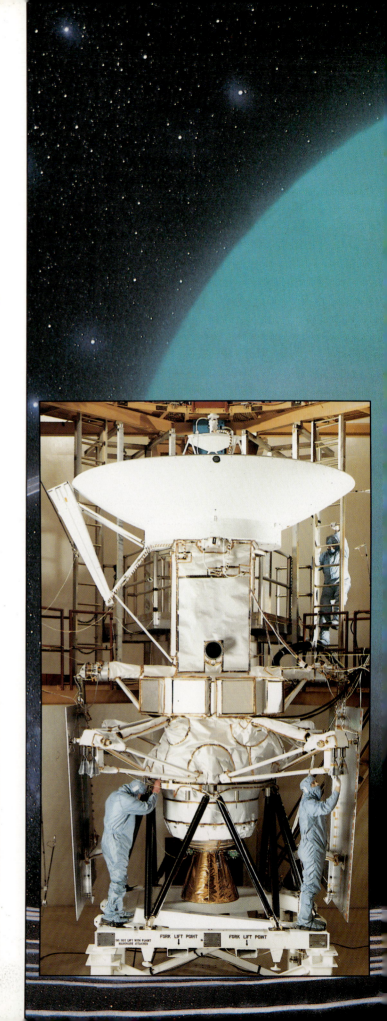

DID YOU KNOW?

● Deep space probes fly so far away from the Sun that there is not enough sunlight to use solar panels to produce electricity for the on-board instruments. Instead, they use nuclear generators.

● During Voyager 2's tour of the planets from 1977 to 1989, the craft flew 7 billion km (4.43 billion miles) and photographed Jupiter, Saturn, Uranus and Neptune.

● The most distant man-made object from Earth is the Pioneer 10 spacecraft, which crossed the planet Pluto's orbit in 1986. In 1991, it will be passed by Voyager 1, which is travelling faster.

MOON MOBILE

The Moon is covered with craters that were formed by dust and rocks crashing into it from space long ago. The parts of the Moon that look flatter and darker are places where molten rock once flowed over the surface covering some of the older craters.

The Moon shines only because it reflects light from the Sun. As viewed from Earth, the shape of the bright part of the Moon changes, depending on where the Earth and Sun are and how much of the bright half of the Moon we can see from Earth.

▶ The Moon's monthly cycle, illustrated by this mobile, begins with the new Moon. To us, this is dark because the Sun is lighting up the half we cannot see. Each night, we see more of the Moon lit up. After a week, one half is bright at night. After two weeks the whole of the Moon is bright. Then less and less is lit up each night until, after 29.5 days, the Moon's cycle is at an end and we have a new Moon once more.

◀ An Apollo astronaut stands on the Moon's cratered surface. With no atmosphere to scatter sunlight, the shadows in the craters are very sharp and the sky is always black.

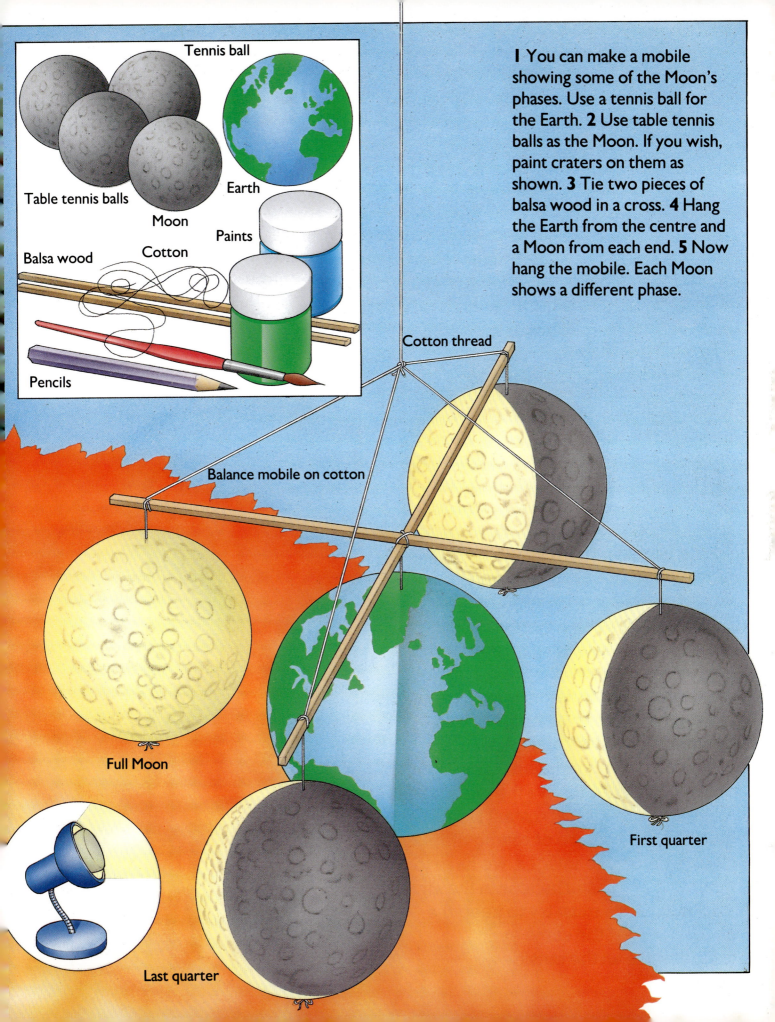

A Trip to the Observatory

This is a true-to-life story. Mark Steele, an author of science fiction books, is collecting background material for his next project. He visits an observatory to learn about galaxies, but his research produces more than just facts and figures. He is one of the first to witness a new cosmic event.

It was a bitterly cold December night. Mark was glad to be going indoors, but even when he closed the observatory door behind him, he noticed that his breath still turned to white clouds of frost.

The observatory director greeted him and explained, "I'm afraid you won't find it any warmer in here because of this." He pointed to an enormous metal framework in the middle of the floor. Above it, huge doors in the roof were sliding open to reveal the velvet black night sky studded with sparkling stars.

The director continued, "This is our one-metre reflector. It's the telescope that we use to look at distant stars and galaxies. To be sure of seeing the clearest possible images, we have to minimise any disturbances in the air. This means we must try to keep the observatory at the same even temperature as the outside air."

He led Mark to a large television set on a desk. "This screen shows the view through the telescope." The screen showed a faint blur of light.

"Is that a star?" Mark asked.

"No," said the director, tweaking the set's controls until the blur was transformed into a beautiful spiral of light with a bulging bright centre. "This is the Andromeda galaxy. It's made up of millions upon millions of stars. In fact, someone has calculated that this particular galaxy contains about 300,000 million stars. It's the closest major galaxy to our own Milky Way, but it's still a long way away – over two million light-years."

"How does the picture get on to the screen? Where does it come from?" asked Mark, producing his notebook.

"Well," said the director. "Light from the galaxy travels through space for over two million years before it reaches the Earth. It travels down through the Earth's atmosphere and enters the telescope at the top of the frame above you. It strikes the mirror at the bottom of the telescope and it is reflected up to a small mirror half-way along the framework. There, it is reflected back down through a hole in the main mirror all the way down to the camera. The camera changes the picture into an electrical signal and feeds it to the television monitor here, where it is changed back into a picture on the screen."

"Of course, using the telescope is only part of an astronomer's work. Astronomers spend a great deal of time analysing the results of their own work and studying the work of other astronomers all over the world."

Mark was writing as quickly as he could. The director continued, "Astronomy is one of the oldest sciences, but it's still changing and still producing new information about the Universe. I'll give you an example. The astronomer's eye is a very poor light detector to place at the end of the telescope and it can't store images. We used to use photographic plates to record images."

"And don't you use photographs any longer?" Mark interrupted.

"We do," the director answered. "But we now have a new, more sensitive detector."

He led Mark across the room to a computer. "The detector is like a computer chip. It changes the image from the telescope into electrical signals that we can feed straight into a computer. The computer can then process the image to show differences in colour and contrast that our eyes aren't sensitive enough to detect."

He pressed a button on the computer keyboard next to the screen. "Our computer system not only stores and processes the telescope images, it also controls the telescope's position."

Mark watched as the telescope glided round to a new position.

"This is a star field in a region of space where new stars are forming," the director said, pointing to the new picture that had appeared on the screen. "By studying these stars we can learn something about our own star, the Sun. We can learn how it formed, how long ago it formed, how long it will last and what might happen to it in the future."

He pressed several keys on the keyboard. The picture changed from a golden yellow colour to a rich mixture of reds, oranges and blues.

"By analysing the energy from the star field, we can tell, for example, how hot it is. The computer has given each temperature a different colour. White and yellow are the hottest and blue is the coolest. We can also make the colours represent other things – brightness, radio energy, speed or direction of movement. So you see there are lots of different ways of looking at planets, stars and galaxies."

Mark nodded. He had plenty of information for his next book.

"Now we have a surprise for you", said the director. "While we were checking the latest batch of images, we discovered a new galaxy that no-one has ever seen before."

He punched a key on the computer and a pale yellow ball appeared on the screen. "This is a special type of astronomical object called a quasar. It's extremely bright, so bright that it swamps the dimmer light from the galaxy around it," the director told him, a note of excitement in his voice.

"We consulted fellow astronomers in Australia and they're checking it with their radio telescope. We can tell a lot about an astronomical object by observing it at different wavelengths. The radio telescope picks up details invisible to our optical telescope."

"You mean, you receive radio messages from these distant quasars?" asked the author.

"Oh yes," the director nodded. "Radio signals pour out of them."

"Any signs of life?"

The director smiled. "Unfortunately not. We occasionally run the radio receptions through a computer to look for anything interesting. Sometimes the computer identifies brief patterns, but nothing that looks as if it had come from an alien being. Sorry I have to disappoint you."

An idea was beginning to hatch in Mark's head. What if a routine analysis of radio signals from a distant galaxy revealed a repeating pattern that looked as if it had come from an intelligent being? What would it look like or sound like? How could the messages locked in the strange signals be decoded and understood? What might they say? What sort of beings might they have come from? Mark thanked the director and left the observatory with his mind full of ideas.

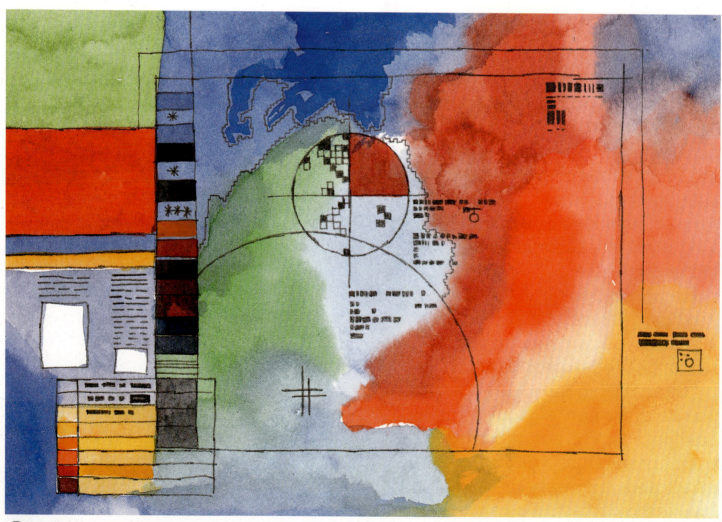

TRUE OR FALSE?

Which of these facts are true and which ones are false? If you have read this book carefully you will know the answers.

1. The scientific study of the stars and planets is called astrology.

2. The zodiac contains more than 14 constellations.

3. The Greek astronomer Ptolemy believed the Earth was at the centre of the Universe. This was called the Ptolemaic System.

4. The planet Uranus was discovered by the astronomer Sir William Herschel in 1781.

5. The reflecting telescope, or reflector, was invented by the Italian astronomer Galileo.

6. Most space probes use solar panels to convert sunlight into electricity. Deep space probes such as Voyager 2 use nuclear power generators because far from the Sun there is not enough light for solar panels to work.

7. By 1988, Soviet and US unmanned space probes had flown past or landed on all of the Solar System's planets.

8. When the Moon comes between the Sun and the Earth it is called a solar eclipse.

9. The Moon shines brightly because it is so hot that it glows.

Answers: 1. False. 2. False. 3. True. 4. True. 5. False. 6. True. 7. False. 8. True. 9. False.

GLOSSARY

● **Atmosphere** is the layer of gases surrounding the Earth.

● **Craters** are bowl-shaped hollows in the surface of a planet or moon. They are caused by lumps of rock called meteorites crashing into the surface.

● **Eclipse** is the covering of one object in the sky by another. For example, when the Moon hides the Sun, this is called a solar eclipse. When the Earth hides the Sun from the Moon, it is called a lunar eclipse.

● **Galaxies** are star systems. Each is held together by the gravitational attraction between the hundreds of millions of stars in the system. Our Solar System belongs to a galaxy called the Milky Way.

● **M20** is another name for the Trifid Nebula. M20 means that it was the 20th item listed in the catalogue of French astronomer Charles Messier in 1781.

▼ The Herschel Telescope in its mountain-top dome where the atmosphere is clear.

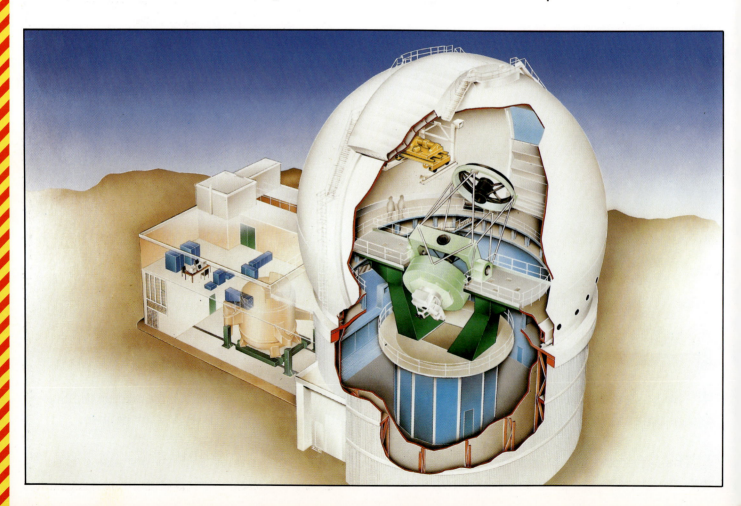

▲ The Great Globular Cluster, a type of galaxy of about half a million stars.

● **Nebula** is a cloud of gas and dust in space where stars form.

● **Orbit** is the path followed by an object, such as a planet, as it revolves around a larger object, such as a star. One orbits the other because of the force of gravity pulling them together.

● **Quasars** are the most distant objects that can be seen from Earth and are probably galaxies whose centres have exploded.

● **Solar System** is the Sun, the planets and the other objects that orbit it.

TELESCOPE TIMECHART

1608 The telescope is thought to have been invented by a Dutch lens maker, Jan Lippershey.

1610 Galileo makes a telescope and begins telescopic astronomy.

1663 The idea of a reflecting telescope is suggested by James Gregory.

1668 Sir Isaac Newton makes the first reflecting telescope.

1824 A telescope in Dorpat, Estonia, is the first to be fitted with a clockwork motor to allow it to follow the motion of the stars.

1845 The third Earl of Rosse uses his 91 cm (36 inch) reflector to discover the spiral shape of galaxies.

1930 The Schmidt telescope is invented to photograph large areas.

1937 The first radio telescope is designed and built by the US engineer Grote Reber.

1962 The first orbiting observatory, OSO-1, is launched.

1990 Hubble Space Telescope is launched.

INDEX

astrology 4, 6
astronomers 4, 6, 8, 10
atmosphere 12, 16, 18

binoculars 10

constellations 6
Copernicus 9
craters 12, 22

Earl of Rosse Telescope 31
Earth 4, 6, 16, 18, 22
eclipse 12

galaxies 12, 18
Galileo 9
gravity 9

Herschel, Sir William 9
Hubble Space Telescope 18, 19

Jupiter 12, 20

Kepler, Johannes 9

Lippershey, Jan 31

Magellan space probe 20
Mars 9, 20
Messier, Charles 30
Milky Way 30
Moon 4, 7, 12, 22

nebula 4
Neptune 20
Newton, Sir Isaac 9

observatories 10, 14
orbit 20
Orbiting Solar Observatory 18

planets 4, 6, 12, 20
Pluto 20
Ptolemaeus, Claudius 4

quasars 16, 31

radio telescopes 16, 17
reflecting telescope 9, 11
refracting telescope 11
Royal Observatory, Greenwich 14

Saturn 12, 20
Skylab 18
Solar System 20
space probes 20
Space Shuttle 18, 19
stars 4, 6, 11, 12, 18
Sun 4, 6, 7, 9, 12, 13

telescope
    Anglo-Australian 14
    Schmidt 14, 31
    Space 18, 19
telescopes 9, 10, 11, 12, 16, 17, 18
Trifid Nebula 4

Uranus 9, 20

Venus 20
Voyagers 1 and 2 20

zodiac 6